Seasons Of The Soul

Payal Singh

BookLeaf
Publishing

India | USA | UK

Made with ❤ on the BookLeaf Publishing Platform
www.bookleafpub.in
www.bookleafpub.com

To those who love deeply,

To those who find beauty in the simplest of moments,

And to those who have weathered every season of the heart with grace–

This book is for you.

May these words be a reminder that love, like nature,

Grows, changes and blossoms again.

And know that love will find you at the right time, in the right place and with the right person.

Acknowledgement

This collection would not have been possible without the love, encouragement and inspiration of those around me. To my family and friends, thank you for your unwavering support and belief in my words, even during moments of doubt. Your presence in my life is the foundation on which these poems have been built.

To all the dreamers, lovers and seekers who have walked into my life – thank you for leaving your mark. Your stories, your laughter and your heartbreak have shaped these verses, weaving together the threads of nature, romance and reflection that fill these pages.

I would also like to express my gratitude to the readers – you are the reason these words come alive. May you find a reflection of your journey here, and may these poems speak to your heart, as they did to mine.

Lastly, a heartfelt thanks to the natural world – for the moonlit nights, the whispering trees and the beauty of every changing season – a constant reminder that life, in all its forms, is poetry.

Preface

Seasons of the Soul is a journey through the landscapes of the heart, where love, nature and the mysteries of life intertwine in rhythmic harmony. Each poem is like a season, capturing the fleeting beauty of moments that define who we are – moments of love and longing, reflection and renewal, struggle and serenity.

These verses invite you to walk through moonlit forests, sit beside the warmth of campfires, fall in love beneath twinkling stars and find comfort in the whispers of a gentle breeze. They speak to the parts of us that crave connection, wonder at the beauty of the natural world and seek meaning in both joy and sorrow.

As you read, I hope you find fragments of your own story within these pages – the times you've soared, the moments you've stumbled and the quiet spaces where hope flickered like a lone star in the night sky. Let these poems be a reflection of your seasons, a reminder of the constancy of change and the beauty that emerges when we embrace each transformation.

Welcome to this journey of the soul, where each poem serves as a reminder that, just as the seasons change, so too do our hearts – always growing, always evolving.

1. Flicker of Hope

When night descends,
Lying beside the window's edge,
You gaze into the silent sky,
Reflecting on the hours gone by.

On a moonless, clouded night,
Only one star graces your sight–
Faint and dim, yet standing still,
Alone, above the quiet hill.

One lone star in the darkened sky,
Softly flickering, pale and shy.
And yet, somehow, your weariness fades,
A smile settles as all worry decays.

With hope renewed and dreams alight,
You drift to sleep beneath the night.
For what is the power of one dim star?

To heal, to soothe from afar–
It carries you through until dawn,
Where strength returns and doubts are gone.

2. Petals of You

Whenever I see a Gulmohar tree,
The flowers remind me of you.
Just as you set me free,
The winds set them free too.
A petal fell on me, feeling like a kiss from
you.
You might not understand this glee,
But trust me, what I speak is true.

3. As the Night Fell

As the night fell,
Birds returned back
To their dwell.

Bats took over the sky,
The owl's hoot
Took over the vibes.

Snails came out
In search of food,
And deer stepped out
Into the woods.

Water stood still,
Reflecting the white light
Of the moon.

Stars twinkled in the sky
Like diamonds
Of some merchant
Who just passed
The village nearby.

Those scared
Of the dark and theft,
Worried someone could loot
Gems that were left.

Scared of ghosts on the nearest
Peepal tree,
Every time he shivered
As the breeze swayed.

Who could ever tell
He was not alone?
The only one awake
As the night fell.

4. Moi Aussi, Je t'aime

Days have passed, and so have nights
I don't know how time with you flies.

I still remember, not so long ago,
When I saw you walk in your flow.

All I wanted to say was just hello,
But you were far, and I had to let go.

Five months and some days have passed,
Here we are together; it didn't seem much of
a task.

You always say it was destined for us to meet,
Now isn't that sweet?

You have no idea how you make me complete,
That all my fears become obsolete.

I still remember the day
What you knew in French to say.

When you said 'Bonjour' means hello,
'Merci' means sorry, though it's not so.

And when you said 'Je t'aime' with some
hope,
All I could think of was some stupid joke.

You thought I ignored it, but I didn't;
All I could do was just not guess the hint.

You had to point it out in disappointment,
But what can I do? That's how I am in my
enchantment.

That's why when you said 'Te amo' to give it a
second try,
'I don't know Spanish', is what I replied.

5. Forest's Embrace

Under the moon's quiet gaze,
In the forest's midnight haze,
Sitting on the mountain's crest,
In the campfire light, we find our rest.

The marshmallows toast as flames rise high,
While shadows flicker beneath the sky.
A lion's roar, a distant call,
The forest whispers to us all.

The stars above, the earth below,
In this sacred space, hearts grow.
'This is where your soul takes flight',
A gentle voice said, beneath the moon's light.

6. Priceless

Seeing a person in your dreams every night is
common,
But seeing that person standing by your side
in reality is rare,
But knowing he is going to stand there all his
life is priceless.

Caring for someone is common,
Getting affection from the same person is
rare,
But caring and showing affection to each
other even during fights and
misunderstandings is priceless.

Holding someone's hand in spring is common,
That person holding back your hand in bloom
is rare,
But not leaving your hand on stormy winter
nights is priceless.

Loving someone is common,
Being loved by the same person is rare,
But striving for your love and wanting to be
in love with the same person forever is
priceless.

Saying 'I love you' is common,
Hearing it back is rare,
But if both are meaning it, then it's priceless.

'We became friends' is common,
'We had a crush on each other' is rare,
But 'we fell in love with each other and want
to be together forever' is priceless.

7. The Gulmohar Tree

It started with the rains
When water quenched the thirst
Of a small seed in my lane.
The seed then grew higher and higher,
Showing its vein.

Lush green in colour,
Leaves dancing to the tune of the breeze,
Nature's own art, if one had eyes,
They could see it for free.

Slowly, winds take the clouds away,
Making a sapling a tree.
As winter arrives,
Now is the time to thrive.

All its leaves turn yellow,
But only fall
When the air blows.

The tree looks more or less dead,
But wait a minute, my love,
Summer is still ahead.

Summer brings orange blossoms
On the dead branches, I'm not a liar,
Which makes the tree look handsome
Like it was on its own blazing fire.

What an artist is my mother,
That gives one single tree
Three different colours,
Just to make it look fuller.

As clouds take over the sun,
Rains are back,
Flowers fall by getting drenched for fun,
It's painted back in green.

As the cycle goes on,
Every evening,
I simply stand in my lane
In admiration, singing
For all the beautiful colours you bring.

8. To Love Again

To be honest, yes, I'm scared,
Haunted by past wounds, I'm unprepared.
Somehow, I began to hate the colour red,
But when I met you, holding your hand
instead,

All I wanted was to close my eyes and leap,
Trusting you with secrets I tried to keep.
My fears began to fade as we drew near,
Looking into your eyes made everything clear.

You gave me strength, a gentle push to
believe,
That love can heal and hearts can still receive.
To start again, with you, my heart's request—
A chance to love anew and give my best.

9. Snowdrop

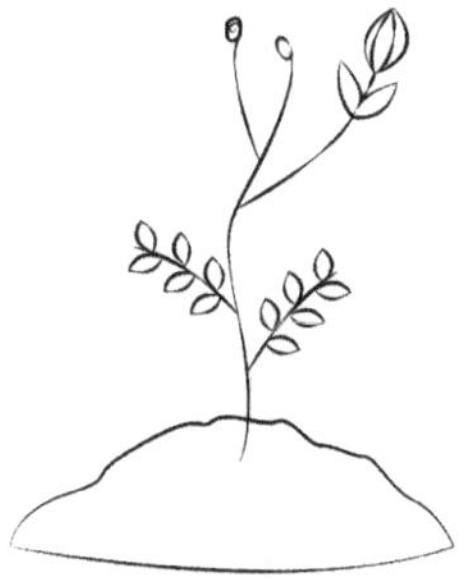

Every morning when I open the window,
All I see is thick white snow.
All the colours are gone, even when I rest,
My head on the pillow, yearning for the best.

Oh, spring, where are you?
Why can't I see a sign, not even a hue?
Not even a seldom bloom in view.

When will the colours return?
When will the sweet breeze blow?
When will the snow melt on the fern?

I hope tomorrow brings a new day,
When a fresh snowdrop will grow,
And I'll dance in glee and gay.

10. The Way I've Loved You

How can I ever truly describe
The depth and breadth of my love for you?
I've loved you under the gentle moonlight,
And through every solitary night.

I've adored you as the sun dipped low,
And in the early dawn's soft glow.
I've cherished you under clear blue skies,
And when the clouds had said their goodbyes.

I've felt you close when you were near,
And clinging to your memory in my fear.
How can words ever truly convey
The way I've loved you, day by day?

11. Echoes of the First Rain

That day when the first raindrop fell,
Not enough to quench my thirst,
Yet my heart kept saying, 'This is just the
first'.

Dry and parched was the soil,
Waiting for the rain amidst all the turmoil.

Just with one hope, I kept looking above,
But not a single cloud moved, even now.

Not knowing why, my heart felt it would rain,
But that was the only ray of hope
In that dry terrain.

Then, from somewhere, a wind came gushing,
Making a furious sound,
But to my ears, it felt as if nature was singing.

Trees danced to its tune,
It was way past noon.

It started to rain,
And it felt that the earth was freed of its pain.

Looking at which, my heart said,
'Always keep the last hope alive,
Or else you'll just become a living dead'.

12. If Only I Had the Power

If only I had the power–
I'd unravel my heart, piece by piece,
To show you every shadow of pain
That echoes when you cease.

If only I had the power,
I'd show you the nights spent in empty spaces,
Where time bends in the silence of your
absence,
And joy returns with the memory of your
face.

If only I had the power,
I'd turn back the stars to the moments we
shared,
To replay the flickers of light we kindled,
Before time dared to tear.

If only I had the power,
I'd let you hear the melody my heart hums,
Each beat a song when you care,
A symphony when you come.

If only I had the power,
I'd capture each breath and every glance,
And etch them into the sky,
So we'd live forever in love's trance.

13. Under the Willow Tree

Sitting under the willow tree,
I always wanted to be free.
Watching the birds chirp and fly,
So happy, singing, soaring high.

All I wanted was to flee with them,
To rise and dip, to twist and stem.
Their freedom made my heart beat fast,
Wishing for courage like theirs to last.

They live each moment, carefree and bold,
Unfazed by the snow or the coming cold.
The snow may fall, it may come soon,
And summer may lose its glowing moon.

But the freedom they show is pure and true,
Unafraid of what the future might do.
That's how I wish to truly be,
Every time I'm sitting under the willow tree.

14. Love is...

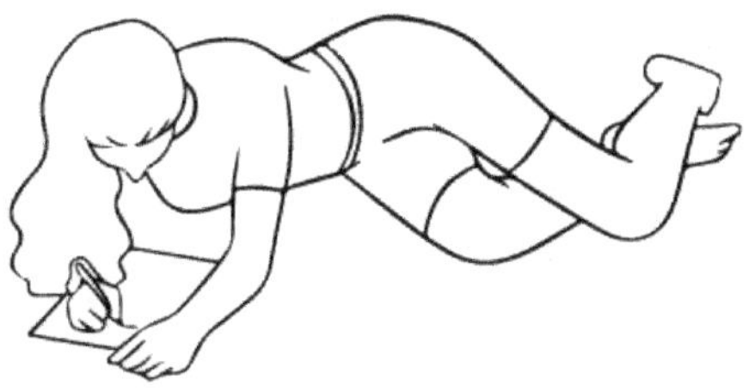

Love is when you can't see them sad or crying,
Or maybe when you apologise for their
mistakes,
Or when you make small sacrifices just to see
them happy.

Love is when they fall in love with you every
day,
Or maybe when they look at you as if it's the
first time.

Love is when they wake up early just to spend
time with you,
Or maybe when they start loving colours
because of you.
Or maybe when you forget the anniversary
but they don't,

Or simply when you stay up late, waiting for
their drowsy night chats to begin.

Love is when they listen to your spoken
words, every time,
Or maybe when they hear your unspoken
words, every time.

15. A Walk with Eros

One day I went on a walk with Eros,
Just to talk.
We spoke about days and nights,
About the gods and their fights.

Soon, he said to me, 'I have to go
To someplace that is not my home,
Yet I must go, for it is my destiny,
Though it is not tiny'.

I asked him,
'Can I see you there? Will we meet again'?
To which he replied,
'No, but I for sure will send someone to take
your care'.

I asked him,
'How will I find him? Where to see'?
He said,
'You don't have to; you'll know my love when
your heart will glee'.

The moment I saw you, my heart skipped a
beat,
Everything sang and danced on its feet.
I really don't know if Eros was talking of this
glee,
But every time I see you, my heart truly flees.

16. As Dusk Settles

As night unfurled its sombre veil,
The world's truths whispered without fail.
In the quiet, my heart couldn't find reprieve,
Each revelation teaches me to grieve.

The deeper I saw into other souls,
The more your virtues began to unfold.
Your love, once a quiet constant truth,
Now echoes as the profound depths of my
youth.

Perhaps it was I who harboured the poison,
Leaving behind a heart fractured and frozen.
A void sprawls where your warmth once lay,
In the chambers where echoes of your loyalty
stay.

No other has shown such steadfast grace,
Or held me close in an earnest embrace.
What fate is this that I must now bear,
To wander lost in open air?

Longing for one who cherished the rains,
Who whispered love in quaint refrains.
Those melodies, once sweet and clear,
Now distant echoes I strain to hear.

Gone are the days of simplicity,
Replaced by layers of complexity.
Time slips by, a relentless thief,
Stealing more than just belief.

I can't condemn you, for the worst has shown,
What I deserved – reaped from the seeds I've
sown.
You set aside all to grant me flight,
A release into the starless night.

Yet tonight, as whispers stir the leaves,
Your voice emerges in the breeze.
A longing plea for absolution's touch,
'My love, forgive me; I've missed you much'.

In the quiet night, your silhouette dreams,
Where apologies flow in silent streams.
'If only sorrow could right the wrongs,
For in your absence, my heart longs'.

17. Why I Love You

How can I ever truly say,
Why do I love you? Let me convey:
Perhaps because you think like me,
A mirrored soul, in sync, we're free.

Or maybe for the things you do,
The feats beyond my reach, it's true.
In spaces where no others tread,
You dance in steps uniquely led.

It might be that I know you're there,
A presence felt when others disappear.
No need for words, you understand,
A rare connection, hand in hand.

Could it be that life with you turned belle?
You caught me each time I fell.
In your eyes, I see shared dreams,
Our goals as one, a single beam.

Or simply, might it be because
We're meant to be, as the universe does?
My soul once searched, now it sees,
In you, I've found my destined peace.

18. The Wonderer

He wondered about places, in search of one–
A place where his heart would sing in fun,
The one that he had imagined all his life,
Reading the book 'An Island Where Treasure
Lied'.
Not one with jewels, gems and gold coins,
But one where peace, solitude and harmony
would join for dine.
A place where the astral body would dance to
the tune of the wind,
And at night, the cricket would sing.

He wanted to attach some sort of wings to fly
up above the sky,
That's all he wanted before he died.
Years passed on, wondering – no such place
was found,
A place where the moon was always round,
Where the stars would shine so bright to light
up the sight.
One day, the search was over.
He found a planet where the water was
covered.
He brought his friends and family; they all
liked it,
And that's how humans built their first
society.

19. Walk Miles

I can't believe
That I was ever
Able to give.
Now that you've gone,
I don't even know
What to talk about anymore.

I was never so
Afraid to walk alone,
But now I'm so used to you–
I can't bear
Even a pinch of loneliness.

What will happen
If you're not mine?
If you leave me to face the end,
I know I won't be fine,
For in my heart,
With you, I want to walk
Miles...

20. Tale of a Chrysanthemum

Once, I asked a Chrysanthemum,
'Winter has approached; all your friends are
now asleep.
Yet here you stand, still smiling wide–
Aren't you afraid of the death that creeps'?
Smiling, she replied with grace,
'Everyone must one day lie beneath the dew,
So why harbour fear for the inevitable night?
Instead, I choose to revel in the morning's
new'.
'Knowing that my end may soon arrive,
I wish to savour each moment under the sun's
glow.

For life is fleeting, a brief, brilliant spark,
And in this brief time, joy is the only truth I
wish to know'.

21. What is Love?

Once, a friend asked me on a quiet day,
'What is love, in its own subtle way'?
I paused, caught in thought,
And here's what I sought:

Love might be when–
You wipe your hands on his shirt without
care,
And he only smiles, knowing he's there.

Love might be when–
Seeing you trapped in life's cage,
He carries your weight, feeling your rage.

Love might be when–
Your smile makes his eyes gleam,
And his laughter feels like a gentle dream.

Love might be when—
You wear his shirt to sleep at night,
And in that, he finds his own delight.

Love might be when—
You can't eat what's on your plate,
So he leaves it too, as he patiently waits.

Love might be when—
He picks up the spoon with gentle grace,
Feeding you, giving hunger no space.

Love might be when—
He holds each promise close,
But always makes room for more, even those
unspoken.

Love might be when—
He stands by your side, through wrong and
right,
A quiet pillar in the darkest night.

Love might be when—
He gives his last coin without a thought,

Not for gain, but for what your happiness has
brought.

Love might be when–
Seeing your tears, he cries in return,
Not for the pain, but for the lessons we learn.

Love might be when–
His trust in you runs deep and blind,
A treasure so rare, it's hard to find.

Love might be when–
He knows your heart, every beat and turn,
No need for words, just the bond you both
earn.

Love might be when–
In endless conversations, he chooses you,
Because with you, there's always something
new.

And when all was said,
I simply replied:
'Love is so vast and so fine,
It slips beyond words, even mine'.

22. Dusk

I love the shade of dusk
When the Sun's going down,
And it's not all around.
Orange is blended with grey,
And all of a sudden fades.
Though the sky is still bright,
A little chirping bird flies back to its home.
No part of the day soothes me like this,
As if it is the place where I fit.
Its beauty can't be described in words,
But here I am, trying to do a little work.

23. If Time Were Sold

What if time were merchandised in little
shops?
I'd buy hours just for us–
To soar high like kites in skies so vast and
blue,
To discover what it feels like to live aloft, just
me and you.

I'd purchase moments to dive deep beneath
the sea,
To explore its silent depths and all its
mysteries.
I'd secure nights to sit beside you under starlit
skies,
Where we could gaze at constellations
without any guise.

I'd invest from dawn to dusk and back again,
Spending each borrowed hour where our
stories begin.
I'd even turn back time to when you weren't
near,
To relive each second and hold those
moments dear.

If only I could buy such time, yet it's so
priceless and rare–
Even the wealthiest cannot purchase air.
For we're allotted just a fleeting share,
Like grains of sand slipping through fingers
bare.

So let's vow to cherish every tick and tock,
Come close, let's let the remaining moments
dock.
And when we look back, let it be with glee,
For in these seconds, we've made our own
eternity.

24. Soaring Release

How long can he endure,
With such a haul upon his back?
Why does he cling to it,
Continuing on this gruelling track?

Can he not see his burdened spine,
Living life akin to a bee–
Endlessly toiling, seeking nothing
But the honey of weary, ceaseless spree?

Do not his shoulders scream in pain?
What could possibly be the gain?
How far will he go,
How long can he sustain this show?

Nature itself weeps for him,
Wounded by the sight of his grim.
It's time to change the tale, shed those blues,
Break free from chains; there's nothing to
lose.

Let him soar above, beyond the skies,
Where freedom calls, where his spirit flies.
Let him find the place where he can breathe,
Unburdened, unbound, finally at ease.

25. Why Do We Wonder?

Sometimes I wonder why–
Why day turns to night,
Why shadows fight the light,
Why does a child cry before dreams unfold,
Why does one give up before becoming bold?
Why does the sky wear its endless blue,
While water hides its hue?
Why do stars keep secrets in the dark,
And why can't I love you where the heavens
arc?
Why do roses grow with thorns,
And why can't we stop grieving once love is
torn?

But of all the mysteries, one I know true–
Why is love so hard to find?
Perhaps because it's blind,
Or it waits, hidden, beneath the view.

26. Let It Go

Walking down a moonlit street,
Cursed and weary, dragging your feet.
Fatigue sets in; you've never felt so weak,
The night seems darker than the solace you
seek.

Tumbling, tumbling,
Down you fall,
No hand to catch you,
No voice to call.

The stars seem distant, fate feels cold,
Loneliness lingers, taking its hold.
But let your wounds begin to heal,
This is the moment, and it's real.

Now is the time to mend your heart,
To stop the hurt, to make a new start.
Close the door to yesterday's sorrow,
Embrace the dawn of a brighter tomorrow.

Tonight's the night to release the foe,
To rise again and let it go.
Under the stars, your heart will mend,
For in the night, even broken things bend.

27. Whispers of Venus

I've never felt this before–
Why am I so bored?
Never wanted to give up,
But this time, passion has stirred up.

I pray to the stars above,
To show me what the future holds in love.

It feels different, deep in my core,
But will it heal my heart
And open the door?

You were right,
The future is drawn,
So what is there to fear at dawn?

I thank you for lighting my way,
But still, I wonder–
Will he stay or stray?

Then Venus whispered in a gentle tone,
'Fear not, for you are never alone.
For love has found you, pure and bright,
It's written in the heavens; your fate is light.
I won't leave you; love is true–
Your heart and his are destined to bloom'.

28. The Life of a Star

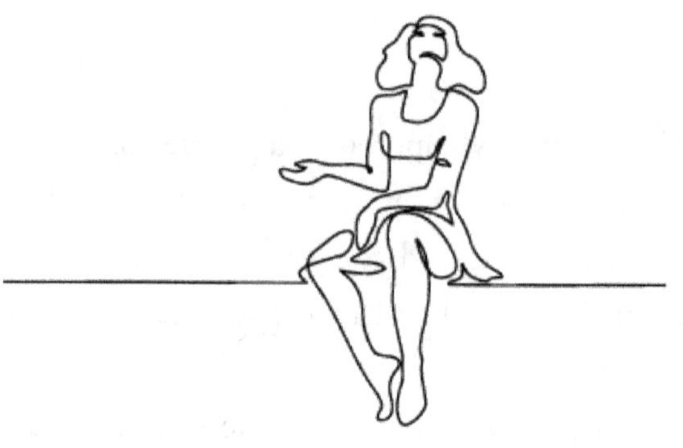

Life is a star–
When it's born,
It shines bright, even
Though it's far.

In its teens,
It burns to enlighten lives,
And that's why
It gleams in the darkest skies.

In its youth,
It destroys itself just to
See someone smile,
Even if only for a little while.

And in its final breath,
Under its light, a lost shepherd
Finds the path ahead,
Led away from dread.

Even on its tomb,
It grants wishes in the night,
Bestowing a boon.

Hats off to the star,
Who serves its whole life for you,
And is never thanked,
For all that it selflessly gives and renews.

29. Eternal Flame

After weeks apart, we met again,
Blazing with anger, words spilt in vain.
Not knowing what I was saying,
But when I met you,
Your embrace worked like a drop of dew–
A soothing touch for my weary heart.

My anger melted as you held me tight,
Though I sat in silence,
Your presence filled the night.
Holding my hand, sitting close,
I remembered all the moments I missed you
most.

When you lifted me up, I felt loved,
And when your lips met mine,
I knew – you were truly mine.

If I could rest my head on your chest,
Listening to your heartbeat all night long,
I'd dance to its rhythm,
Lost in its song.
Is it crazy that even after you're gone,
I still feel your presence lingering on–
Like an eternal flame, forever strong?

30. As The Sun Bows Low

As the sun bows low,
Birds trace paths back to nests they know.
Candles flicker into life,
Scattering the edges of night.

Sheep huddle close in the cooling air,
Aware, somehow, that night is near.
Flowers dip their heads toward the earth,
Their pride was subdued but still of worth.

An owl hoots under the starry dome,
Watching the universe from its lofty home.
Fireflies dance to silent tunes,
Their lights weaved through the dusk's
monsoons.

A traveller pauses to embrace the rest,
For tomorrow beckons, a new quest–
To explore beneath the expanding sky,
As the world spins and night drifts by.

31. A Living Gem

Some days are simply better than others,
While some feel like walking on fragile
eggshells.
If only I could command Apollo to rise,
Oh, how wise that would be!

If only I could ask Poseidon to unleash his
might,
To clash with the mountains, stir the seas,
And summon quakes that would bring back
the light.

If only I could persuade Athena to lend her
shield,
To crush the pain, the struggles I must wield.

If I had the power to convince even one,
My world would shimmer – a living gem
under the sun

32. Never Leaving You

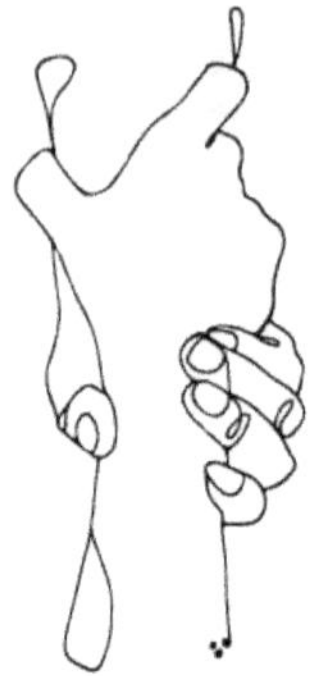

Though the leaves have fallen,
And the blooms have withered away,
Though winter's breath chills the air,
And the light begins to fray–

Even when water turns to ice,
Still, your tears fall like gentle rain.
It's a sorrow that lingers with you,
But why do you think I am far from view?

Look within, beyond the frost,
And you will find me, never lost.
I was always there, in your heart's quiet song,
With you, never leaving, where I belong.

33. As the Night Dawned

As the night dawned,
It comforted me with moonlight,
The stars twinkled just for me.
Years had passed,
Since I last heard the wind sing.
It was thee,
To solace me;
Though could not be touched,
Yet ought to be felt.
Is this the love thou
Speak of?
Doth it make thee feel the same?
Dreamy is this night,
Lovely is its sight.

Leave the ado of the world,
Come hither,
I'll be waiting for thee
Until the night dawns anew.

34. Sometimes

Sometimes when you think I'm looking away,
I can see you staring.
Sometimes when you think I can't hear you,
I can hear your breath whispering.
Sometimes when you're unable to speak,
I can still catch your phrases singing.
I wish I could tell you how I'm feeling
When these little things
Just happens sometimes.

35. The Dark Before Dawn

All my life, I feared being left behind,
Alone, with nothing but this anxious mind.
A fear so vast, a mountain looked small,
So dark, the night seemed brighter than all.
So deep, the ocean's trench felt shallow,
This monster inside casts a mighty shadow.

It haunted me like a beast of the night,
A monster greater than any god's might.
As it dug deeper, I struggled to breathe,
Life felt like it was slipping beneath.
Too tired to carry this weight, I couldn't walk,
Burdened by this fear, unable to talk.

But then I remembered my mother's say–
'Night is darkest just before the break of day'.
And to my surprise, her words rang true,
I found the key that was always in view.

The key was simple, always present near,
But I was too blinded by darkness to hear.
So let me share this with you today:
I choose you, even if you choose not to stay.
I don't need to impress or plead for you to be,
I'm here, in this moment, finally free.

www.ingramcontent.com/pod-product-compliance
Lightning Source LLC
Chambersburg PA
CBHW061708130726
47996CB00006B/2217